GW00400868

HOW TO
OVERCOME
DISTRACTION
IN PRAYER

—

FR ED BROOM, OMV

All booklets are published
thanks to the generosity of the supporters
of the Catholic Truth Society

First published 2024
by The Incorporated Catholic Truth Society,
42-46 Harleyford Road, London SE11 5AY.
Tel: 020 7640 0042. *www.ctsbooks.org*

ISBN 978 1 78469 765 5

Contents

For God so loved the world that he gave his one and only Son, that whoever believes in him shall not perish but have eternal life.

(*Jn* 3:16)

Noise and Distractions:
A Ubiquitous Modern Phenomenon

The story of Elijah in the Bible tells of how the prophet fled for his life when the wicked Queen Jezebel and her weak husband, King Ahad, determined that he must be put to death, and as quickly as possible. After challenging the false prophets of Baal and winning the challenge, he had summarily put them to death by slitting their throats, hundreds of them, with none saved. Aware of his precarious situation, Elijah fled speedily to spare his life. When he had completed a day's journey on foot, God sent an angel who gave him bread to eat. After eating the bread twice, Elijah walked forty days and forty nights to the holy mountain of Horeb, where he sought the presence of God.

At Horeb, Elijah learnt that the Lord God could not be found in the earthquake, nor the thunder, nor the storm; rather, God's presence was manifested in the quiet and gentle wind, the soft and sweet breeze. (See *1 K* 19:1-13.)

In the modern world, especially in the populous cities, noise is part and parcel of the living milieu. Inevitable and unavoidable. The following personal anecdote, about my first four years in Rome, amply illustrates this point.

I had the blessing to study there for seven years, which joyfully culminated in my ordination under the hands of Pope St John Paul II (25th May 1986). I enjoyed the studies, liked the camaraderie of my fellow Oblate brothers, enjoyed the exquisite Italian cuisine, and especially was enamoured with prayer, the many Rosaries and the Holy Sacrifice of the Mass.

However, now already in my late sixties, I can honestly say that never did I live in a place where I was exposed to such constant and profuse noise. As well as being in the middle of the city, our house of formation was connected to a busy Roman Parish, St Elena. The irony is that the founder of the Oblates of the Virgin Mary (my religious order) stated that we oblates were called to be contemplatives in the house and apostles outside.

The following – an explanation, not a complaint – is a list of the many noises and distractions that my sixty fellow seminarians and I were exposed to. My room overlooked the Via Casilina, buzzing with people coming and going, talking and calling out to each other. The street was constantly busy with passing cars, buses, taxis, and motorcycles, but loudest were the mopeds that when motorised to full capacity could explode your eardrums.

Finally, adjacent to the street, believe it or not, were train tracks on which trains sporadically passed by.

Inside the house of formation could be heard a loud-speaker, usually paging a priest to attend a sick person or hear a confession. There were no mobile phones, but the landline phones could be heard ringing often. On the other side of our building was a courtyard. Almost daily, children would come to play football on the concrete pavement, cheering loudly at every goal.

There was also the church bell, which would chime at a certain hour. And, of course, the bells of consecration could be heard loud and clear. Finally, since, due to lack of space, rooms were shared by two seminarians, there was the noise that accompanies different lifestyles.

I survived in spite of all this rather constant noise, but as a consequence I appreciate silence all the more. In the absence of a blessing, one appreciates the blessing all the more when attained.

The relevance of this personal account of mine to our topic is that distractions can be overcome with the grace of God and the collaboration of a human agent. One of the chief remedies for a life of distraction, a life of dissipation, and a life of noise and clatter is the cultivation of a serious prayer life. In fact, the opposite of distraction and dissipation is the idea of 'recollection'.

Silence and Recollection
in the Old Testament

From the beginning of revelation – that is, the Old Testament Scriptures – the foundation on which prayer is built is one of silence and listening. Again and again, we see the Word of God point to silence as the ideal place to meet God.

Abram

In silence and recollection, Abram prostrated himself before the face of the Lord, and then the Lord spoke to him. He would be the Patriarch of the Jewish people (*Gn* 17:3-8).

Moses

On the heights of the mountain, Moses, the great friend of God to whom God would speak face to face, encountered the Lord and was given the stone tablets containing the Ten Commandments (*Ex* 20:1-17).

Elijah

As mentioned earlier, Elijah did not encounter God in the fire, the earthquake, the thunder or the lightning. Rather, Elijah encountered God in the quiet and gentle breeze (*1 K* 19:1-13).

Samuel

Living in the Temple of Shiloh next to Eli, the priest, Samuel heard the voice of God more than once. Eli advised that the next time this happened, Samuel should respond to the voice of the Lord with humility, in these words: "Speak, O Lord, for your servant is listening" (*1 S* 3:1-10).

The psalmist (David)

"His delight is in the law of the Lord, and on his law he meditates day and night" (*Ps* 1:2). The calm praying of the Psalms can dissipate worldly distractions and give peace and calm to the modern man and woman in their troubled and anxious hearts.

God's creation

The world was created in six days. The seventh day God declared to be a day of rest (see *Gn* 1:1-31; *Gn* 2:1-3). This is a day of rest from physical labour. But it is also a day in which we rest in the Lord through prayer, attendance at Holy Mass where we listen to the Word of God, and in silence talk to our Eucharistic Lord in the very depths of our heart.

Hosea

The romantic poet Hosea, using an image of lovers, says that God will take us out into the desert and there he will speak to our heart (see *Ho* 2:14-23). Indeed, the desert is viewed symbolically as a place of struggle. However, it is also portrayed as a place of silence, propitious for entering into prayer and deeper union with God.

The Life of Jesus: A Model for Silence, Prayer and Recollection

The entire public life of Jesus can be divided into intense activity, prepared for by deep silence and recollection. This has served as a model for the lives of many saints, especially those who chose the religious life. The desert fathers (and mothers) dedicated most of their lives to giving themselves up to silence, in which they encountered God and battled fiercely, with the help of his grace, to conquer their enemy, the devil.

Contemplation of the life of Jesus, who is truly "the Way, the Truth, and the Life", can serve as a model and stimulus for us to imitate in our daily sojourn and pilgrimage towards our eternal homeland. Distractions can indeed be conquered if we contemplate the deep and fecund silence of the life of Jesus.

Silence of Bethlehem

One of the most well-known and loved Christmas hymns is "Silent Night". In the quiet of that solemn and holy night, the Christ-Child, the Creator of the universe, was born. As Venerable Fulton J. Sheen noted with his famed perspicacity: "The Creator of the universe had nowhere to be born in his own creation." No words from the cave of Bethlehem were recorded in Sacred Scripture, but we know that in the midst of the surrounding fields, because of the silence and recollection, the angelic choir could be heard singing, "Glory to God in the highest and peace to people of good will" (*Lk* 2:1-15).

Holy family life

Pope St Paul VI, speaking in 1964, highlighted these hidden years of Jesus – thirty long years – about which there is absolute silence. As the holy pontiff pointed out, Jesus prayed, worked and obeyed – all of this in an atmosphere of profound and fertile silence. Indeed, how very eloquent this silence was and still is. Contemplation of the private life of Jesus in Nazareth has catapulted some of the saints into a state of ecstasy. At the same time, we can imagine the Holy Family at the dinner table enjoying a lively conversation about the work they had accomplished that day, the needs of their neighbours, of which they would have been keenly aware, and the good they saw in others. It is unthinkable to imagine the Holy Home of Nazareth bombarded by arguments, clamour, clashes and loud noises. These would militate fiercely against a truly contemplative and joy-filled life.

St Joseph

There is no doubt that St Joseph is and always will be the greatest of all saints – named Protodulia, "the first in veneration", by some scholars. Indeed, a fascinating fact about the glorious St Joseph is that Sacred Scripture has not recorded even one word uttered from his mouth. This does not, of course, mean that this holy patriarch, the foster-father of the Child Jesus, did not speak. However, St Joseph's silence in Scripture could not be more eloquent. It speaks of maintaining a time of silence for prayer, secure against any form of distractions. Moreover, St Joseph proved, by his silent actions, his sincere love for Jesus, Mary and the heavenly Father, as well as those with whom he came in contact. And, lastly, his silence was part of his profound humility. May the silence of St Joseph dispel the distractions of our daily life!

Forty days and nights of desert silence

After his baptism in the River Jordan, Jesus, compelled by the Holy Spirit, spent forty days and forty nights in the desert, where he was absorbed in silence, where he prayed, fasted and was in communion with his heavenly Father. This culminated in Jesus's great struggle, and the ultimate victory that he had over his enemy – Satan, the devil, the enemy of our human nature (see *Mt* 4:1-11). If in our lives we are agitated, distracted and pulled in many different directions, how likely we are to become easy

prey to the devil and his wily deceptions! A distracted
person pulled in many directions is divided and can
easily lose both purpose and focus in their life. In a very
real sense, like Jesus and his sojourn of forty days in
the desert, we all need our own desert experience. The
Catholic Church offers us this opportunity every time
we enter into the holy season of Lent. Lent is a time
to flee from worldly distractions and acquire a spirit of
recollection, reflection, meditation and contemplation in
union with Jesus, who is truly our model – "the Way, the
Truth, and the Life". At its conclusion, we are likely to
want to beg for the grace to live out this spirit of prayer in
our daily life during all the seasons of the year.

Night of mountain silence

Jesus spent the whole night in silence and intimate
conversation with his heavenly Father before choosing
the twelve that he wanted to be his close friends and
co-workers (see *Lk* 6:12-16). How important it is for
us to have silence, without distractions, so as to think
clearly when making important decisions that may affect
the rest of our lives. Being distracted at such times could
turn out to be catastrophic. When making a critical
decision, we need silence to allow for reflection and
proper discernment, culminating in prudent and correct
actions. If Jesus felt a real need for silence and prayer
to choose the right men to carry out his mission – his

apostles – how much more do we need silence and prayer when faced with weighty decisions?

Early morning prayer in a quiet place

In the Gospel of St Mark, Chapter One, the Evangelist portrays a typical day in the public life of Jesus. Once Jesus engaged in his active ministry, he did not let the grass grow under his feet; he moved with alacrity from one activity to the next, wasting no time. G.K. Chesterton said that following the public life of Jesus was like following a lightning bolt! However, before launching himself unreservedly and unstintingly into his preaching, as well as his service of the poor, the suffering, the sick, and the possessed, Jesus found time to be alone without any external distractions. This is another essential condition for fruitful prayer. Mark's Gospel presents Jesus rising long before dawn, finding a solitary place, and being totally absorbed in prayer. No distractions in the least. The apostles had to track Jesus down and point out to him that the people were looking for him (see *Mk* 1:35-36). Jesus is insinuating that we, who live in such a distracted world, should begin our day early, free from distractions, and experience loving communion with the Lord in prayer.

This can help us, when thrown into the rat race of a distracted world, to maintain calm and peace in the depths of our soul. It is said that in the eye of the storm

18

there is calm; and in a stormy and tempestuous sea, there is a quiet calmness in the lower depths. So can our life be calm and peaceful, if we start off our day like Jesus, being absorbed in prayer.

Silence before King Herod

The wicked King Herod plied Jesus with many questions in an effort to force Jesus to talk to him and carry out some miracle. Keenly aware of the impure motives and intentions of the sensualist King Herod, Jesus did not open his mouth to utter a single word (*Lk* 23:6-11). In this matter, Jesus taught us with his earlier sharp warning: "Do not throw your pearls to the pigs" (*Mt* 7:6). How keenly intelligent it is at times not to open one's mouth when in the presence of cynics, scoffers, and base and worldly minded sensualists!

Silence on the cross

Jesus dies and gives up his spirit to the Eternal Father. We contemplate the silence of death, a very eloquent silence. He who is the Light of the world, he who is the Way, the Truth and the Life, he who is the Saviour of the whole universe lays silently on the bed of the cross; Jesus has died. The death of Jesus points to our own death which will come like a thief in the night. Without allowing yourself any distractions, lift your eyes to contemplate Jesus dead on the cross, having given every drop of his

Precious Blood for your salvation and mine. With deep reverence and recollection, contemplate the love Jesus has for you in his death on the cross. The silence of the death of Jesus.

Silence of the tomb – Holy Saturday

With the Easter Triduum – Holy Thursday, Good Friday and Holy Saturday – we enter into the heart of the Church's liturgical year and into the very heart of Jesus and his love for us. Holy Saturday has the characteristic notes of utmost silence and profound recollection, beckoning us to the avoidance of all earthly and worldly distractions. With the help of Mary, Our Lady of Sorrows, we can meet the challenge of this utmost silence and recollection to relive the passion of Our Lord and Saviour, Jesus Christ. Through her eyes, mind, and heart, distant from the boisterous noises and distractions of the world, we can plumb the depths of the love that Jesus had for us in giving himself as a spotless victim on Calvary for our eternal salvation.

In order for us to come to terms with the reality of distractions, and as a sure means to conquer these many distractions, it helps to constantly call to mind these many instances of Jesus seeking or experiencing silence in the Gospels. This contemplation is not a dead, infertile, useless silence. Quite the contrary: it can foster recollection, helping us remove ourselves from a loud, noisy and distracted world, creating for us a fecund silence filled with the love of our Saviour for all mankind.

Having presented a series of biblical reflections on silence in the Old Testament, and in the New Testament in the lives of Mary and Joseph, and especially in the life and person of Jesus, let us identify some of the key distractions in our modern society. In a process akin to the "name it, claim it, and tame it" guidance used by therapists, we can then proceed to offer a remedy to cope with and conquer some of these distractions.

Distractions from Left and Right

———————

Picking up a book about overcoming distractions in prayer suggests that you want to have a prayer life, a life of communication and communion with God the Father, God the Son and God the Holy Spirit, who created you out of love, so that you can know and love them in this life and rejoice with them for all eternity in heaven.

This chapter describes seven serious distractions to our prayer life that by and large are unrecognised, that are lethal to our relationship with God, and that rob us of our dignity and of our destiny, which is heaven. We need to be aware of these lethal distractions so that we can avoid them and take our prayer life and friendship with God more seriously – and not place our salvation in jeopardy.

1. The presence of the devil

Satan, the devil, "prince of this world" (*Jn* 14:29-31), a "roaring lion seeking whom he can devour" (*1 P* 5:8), Beelzebul (*Mt* 12:24): all these are titles for the devil, who will always be on the lookout to create noise in our lives, to ruffle our feathers, and to rock our boat. In the life of St Anthony of the Desert, we have a striking example of how a holy man, pursuing heroic virtue and authentic sanctity of life, could be disturbed and distracted by the devil. Plunged into the midst of the desert (exteriorly a place of utter isolation and silence), St Anthony was tempted by the devil against the virtue of chastity. After the saint had fought off fierce temptations, the Lord appeared to him. Anthony asked the Lord, "Where were you in the midst of these violent temptations against purity?" The Lord responded that he was there, in the very centre of Anthony's heart.

In light of the experience of St Anthony, therefore, we should not be surprised that, as we strive for holiness and a life of recollection that fosters prayer, the devil – the enemy of our salvation according to St Ignatius of Loyola – will be close by distracting us with constant temptations.

The Book of Sirach reminds us: "If you have decided to follow the Lord, prepare yourself for battle" (*Si* 2:1). Indeed, one of the tactics of the devil is to distract us from the ultimate purpose of our existence, which is to attain the eternal salvation of our soul. The Book of Revelation tells us that the devil knows that his time is short.

Consequently, Satan and his minions will do all they can to distract us from our ultimate end, which is heaven, and in this manner: by lulling us into sin, then into the habit of sin, then to being desensitised to sin, and, finally, to making a treaty with the enemy and enslaving ourselves to sin. If this happens and we die in sin, we will lose the ultimate purpose of our life – heaven – and we will endure the tortures of hell for all eternity. The devil is vicious, malicious and an inveterate liar. Jesus tells us from the beginning that the devil is a liar and a murderer (see *Jn* 8:44).

However, there is one vice that the devil does not have: the vice of laziness. Indeed, Satan and his minions work overtime – 25 hours a day, 8 days a week, 366 days a year – and for one purpose: to distract us from the primary purpose of our life – to get to heaven. In the terms of Ignatian spirituality, the "First Principle and Foundation" states our purpose in life: "We are created to praise God, to reverence God, to serve God, and by means of that to save our souls" (*Spiritual Exercises of St Ignatius of Loyola* # 23 – The First Principle and Foundation). The devil wants us to be distracted and to live out the modern philosophy of the sensualist: "You have one life to live! Live it up! Eat, drink and be merry!"

The ultimate goal and purpose of the devil in reality is to immerse us in a sea of distractions that will mesmerise, hypnotise, dope and drug us into a life of sin – mortal sin, deadly sin. Then the devil convinces us that we have a long life to live, with plenty of time to repent and change, thus lulling and seducing us into a false sense of security that keeps us slaves of mortal sin, distracting us from the real purpose of our lives. Then, upon our death, due to our distractions and our slavery to sin, we lose our immortal soul for all eternity. It is for this reason that Jesus teaches with the greatest clarity that death will come like a thief in the night, and woe to the one who is not prepared.

2. Materialism: the god of money

Another powerful, prevalent and pervasive means of distracting us and preventing us from attaining our final purpose is materialism. How easy it is to become attached to material things, especially in societies that have so much, for example the USA, Europe and the UK. Material possessions are not intrinsically immoral or evil; the problem is how easily we can become attached to them, live for them, and even become slaves to them.

In no uncertain terms, Jesus warns us about the inherent danger in allowing ourselves to become absorbed in, attached to, and enslaved by material goods. The following are clear biblical reminders and injunctions, as well as warnings for us perennially. Jesus, the incarnate Son of God, willingly chose and embraced a life of detachment to encourage us to follow in his footsteps. The following examples of his simple way of life help focus our attention upon the crux of our theme: the danger of being distracted from the "First Principle and Foundation" of our lives, particularly by materialism.

Bethlehem

Jesus willingly chose to be rejected before he was even born. A stable or cave in Bethlehem was his birthplace. A place cold, damp and musty, with cobwebs, the rough wood of the manger, the enveloping dark, possibly the smell of animals – all of these are pale images to describe the reality of the entrance of God himself into our world. The eloquent writer, preacher and evangelist Venerable Fulton J. Sheen explained it in one pithy sentence: "The Creator of the universe had no place to be born in his own creation."

Nazareth

Jesus was brought up and raised in the humble and out-of-the-way town of Nazareth, such an ill-favoured place that Nathanael questioned Philip: "Can anything good come out of Nazareth?" (*Jn* 1:46).

Carpenter by trade

For thirty long years in his private life Jesus did not choose for himself an elegant, extravagant, worldly and famous station in life. Quite the contrary: following in the footsteps of his foster-father, St Joseph, Jesus chose the simple profession of a working man, that of the carpenter.

Followers

Neither did Jesus choose the elite, the most educated or brilliant, to be his followers. Not in the least. Jesus chose simple men – the first four were fishermen – to follow him and carry out his work of redemption.

No fixed abode

Given the modern economic crisis in many parts of the world, homelessness is becoming a more common trial for many societies. Many people today have no set or stable abode. Jesus shared this common lot of the homeless of the world.

On earth, Jesus lived about thirty-three years. During the last three years of his life, known as his public life, Jesus preached, healed and cast out many devils. One might ask, "Where did Jesus live for those last three years of his life?" – a very good question, indeed. He no longer lived in Bethlehem, the place of his birth. Nazareth? Yes, he would visit his Mother and preach there at times. Jerusalem? There was no permanent place there for him, either. In Bethany, Mary, Martha and Lazarus would receive Jesus as a welcome guest when he was in town (see *Lk* 10:38-42), but these were only short visits.

Then where did Jesus live for these three years? We have the response in one of Jesus's short statements: "The foxes have their holes and the birds of the air have their nests, but the son of man has nowhere to lay his head" (*Mt* 8:20). These few words uttered by Jesus evoke a whole lifestyle upon which we are challenged to meditate. The Lord and Creator of the universe truly had no place to call 'home', no fixed abode, after his baptism in the River Jordan and his forty days in the desert. Jesus lived every day with total trust in his heavenly Father and divine providence.

God will provide

In his preaching in the Sermon on the Mount, Jesus challenges us to look at the lilies of the fields and the birds of the air. If the heavenly Father provides for them, will he not provide for us? Are we not more valuable than they? Jesus challenges us not to worry, and does so time and time again in this same context of the Sermon on the Mount. He challenges us not to worry about the food we are to eat or the clothes we are to wear. Jesus even challenges us not to worry about the past, the present or the future – for the simple reason that God, our heavenly Father, will provide. He says: "Seek first the Kingdom of God and his righteousness and all these things will be given to you besides" (*Mt* 6:33-34).

Death on the cross

It is a fascinating fact that Jesus died dispossessed of everything. He had no possessions as he hung upon the cross, except a simple loincloth. His detachment from persons, places, things, honour, wealth, even life itself, was total. He had, quoting St Ignatius of Loyola, a complete "holy indifference" to all except the will of his heavenly Father.

Borrowed tomb

As if this were not enough, Jesus would be buried in a borrowed tomb. St Joseph of Arimathea offered for the burial of Jesus a tomb that he had acquired, most likely for himself or his relatives.

Jesus is teaching us by his words, his actions and, indeed, his whole lifestyle that one of the predominant distractions that we must come to terms with and overcome is the all-pervasive, pernicious and insidious reality of materialism. Quite bluntly, Jesus declared: "You cannot serve both God and money" (*Mt* 6:24). Let us pray, with a keen and constant awareness, that we will not be blinded by the materialistic values that surround and inundate us.

3. Utilitarianism

This word is not commonly used, but the concept is a pervasive influence in distracting us from authentic spiritual values. The philosophy of utilitarianism was promoted by John Stuart Mill and Jeremy Bentham (nineteenth-century political philosophers). Note that there is a clear connection or parallel between materialism and utilitarianism. In brief, utilitarianism maintains that the human person has value only inasmuch as they are economically productive and prosperous. The ultimate goal of life, therefore, is to produce so as to acquire, accumulate and possess material things – to store them up and save them.

Consequences of utilitarianism

Therefore, if we follow this philosophy, the logical conclusions related to human life will be the following, all of which militate directly against the dignity of the human person in many ways.

1. *The baby with Down's syndrome in the womb*. Today, once the medical experts detect that the baby in the womb has an extra chromosome – that is to say, it will have Down's syndrome – the immediate recommendation will be to terminate the life before the child is born. Why? Well, the argument usually goes that such a person will never be able to support themselves or live on their own. They will not be able to have a higher education. If they work, it is likely that they will be able to do only the simplest and most menial of tasks. If they get sick, they will be an economic burden to society and to their families. Better to never enter the world than be a burden. Therefore, modern and technologically advanced societies put pressure on women not to bring these children into the world.

2. *The elderly and the terminally ill*. At the other end of the spectrum, in relation to the elderly and the infirm, there is a militant promotion of euthanasia in many modern societies. One of the common themes is the paramountcy of "quality of life", an argument

that negates the fact that God has a purpose for each life from birth until natural death, and negates the salvific value of suffering, joined with the suffering of Jesus on the cross, for the salvation of immortal souls. Euphemisms spread far and wide with their inherent lies: we hear the practice called "mercy-killing", or "allowing the person to die with dignity", or "putting them out of their misery". Once again, the elderly and those with terminal illnesses are seen as a burden to society and their families. Better to give them an injection to put them to sleep, a sleep from which they will never awaken again. Classical Catholic theology calls this murder! Only God has the right to give life and the right to take life away. As we read in the Book of Job: "Naked I came forth from my mother's womb and naked I return to the earth. The Lord gives and the Lord takes away; blessed be the name of the Lord.... If we accept good things from the Lord, then should we not accept evil?" (*Jb* 1:20; *Jb* 2:10).

3. *The severely disabled.* Then there is the wide range of people who for many reasons are severely disabled, for example the paralysed, those seriously injured in accidents, and those who have suffered strokes or aneurysms. Once again, the quality of life of people like this may be called into question. In some cases, the decision, imbued with the pervasive philosophy of utilitarianism, may be, "Why should

these economically deprived individuals be a drain on society? Better for them not to live. Let's facilitate the practice of euthanasia."

What an enormous distraction from God's truth and charity is the philosophy of euthanasia in the modern world, and how pervasive it really is! It comes as a daughter of materialism and utilitarianism. It is desperately sad that so many people are tainted and blinded to the extent of thinking that what really matters and has value in life is the ability to produce, and so to have, possess, and accumulate.

4. Religious indifferentism

Another prevalent distraction from focusing on our ultimate purpose in life is religious indifferentism. It must be stated from the outset that indifferentism is not the same as indifference. By indifference we understand an attitude of apathy, flippancy and carelessness towards life and religious values and practice. This is not what we are talking about.

Never have we lived in a world with so much information – Google and you have the information you seek in a matter of seconds. However, it must be said that never have we lived in a society with so much confusion in almost all realms of society. This spills over into religious circles, and even into Catholicism. By religious indifferentism is meant the assertion that all religions are equal, that no one religion or philosophy is superior to another. Buddhism, Hinduism, Islamism, Judaism, Protestantism, Catholicism – all these religions are really the same because they all lead to God. Therefore, it does not matter which religion you choose.

How erroneous to say that the prophet Muhammad and Allah the supreme God of Islam are the same as Jesus Christ, the Son of God made man, who came to save us through his incarnation and death on the cross, shedding every drop of his Precious Blood on Calvary for our salvation. These are two totally different belief systems claiming redemption and salvation. They cannot both be true. How injurious it is to God, who is truth itself, to assert that truth and falsehood are indifferent in his sight.

Unfortunately, religious indifferentism is pervasive and pernicious, finding its roots even in the hearts of many people who call themselves Catholics. Without a doubt, never have we lived in a world with so much information, but never have we lived in a world with so much confusion about the truth.

5. Moral relativism

Just as utilitarianism is an off-shoot of materialism, moral relativism is an off-shoot of religious indifference. In April 2005, the brilliant theologian, scholar and future pope Joseph Ratzinger warned us of the danger of what he termed a "dictatorship of relativism" ruling modern life. By this he meant that there are no moral absolutes. Rather, the truth is subject to change. The Greek philosopher Heraclitus stated that the world is in a state of perpetual flux, like a stream in motion. Applied to religion and the moral life, this false philosophy asserts that what may have been the truth in the past is subject to change in the present and the future.

Moral relativism turned out to be one of the most pervasive and pernicious concepts in the 20th century, flowering and blossoming in our modern milieu. One of the key moments which gave the "dictatorship of relativism" momentum, like a boulder dislodged from the top of a mountain, was the publication of the encyclical *Humanae vitae* by Pope St Paul VI in July 1968.

Indeed, if there ever existed a true distraction blinding us from seeing the fullness of the truth, it would be the downright rejection of the teaching in this encyclical.

Humanae vitae

As the result of an erroneous interpretation of the global population explosion, many asserted that action should be taken to limit population growth. As a result of modern technological progress and science, the use of contraception – in other words artificial birth control – was advocated as the most efficacious means to limit the population and save humanity. "The pill" was viewed as the clear solution.

However, contrary to popular opinion, Pope St Paul VI, supported by Bishop Karol Wojtyla, the future Pope St John Paul II, stated clearly in his encyclical *Humanae vitae* that the use of contraception to avoid having children was immoral. In other words, every marital or conjugal act should be open to life. Therefore, any use of contraception is intrinsically disordered.

Controversy erupts

As a result of the publication of *Humanae vitae*, the moral debate exploded into the open. The rapid, overt and widespread diffusion of moral relativism that followed showed just how much this modern heresy had already crept into society and formed how most people, including Catholics, had come to think about moral questions. It was no longer a matter of following Church doctrine, but rather of following what was acceptable to the majority of people, including some Catholic theologians.

One such theologian was the renowned priest professor at Catholic University of America in Washington DC, Charles Curran, who, in defiance of the Pope, stated that this encyclical was not binding in conscience. As a result, the following of one's own personal conscience became the modern theological trend. The real problem was, and still is, that very few persons (even among Catholics) have a well-formed conscience. If one's conscience is cauterised, deformed, suppressed, erroneous, lax or misinformed, then how is it possible to make a correct moral judgement, especially on a matter as serious as bringing new life into the world?

The well-known writer, author and Catholic theologian Dr Scott Hahn described the trend using the term "cafeteria Catholicism". In a cafeteria you can pick and choose your foods – whatever your tastebuds prefer; in a parallel sense, many Catholics have become cafeteria Catholics, picking and choosing whatever teachings of the Church appeal to their spiritual tastebuds. It works something like this: "Heaven, I choose; hell, I discard! Moral permissiveness, I choose, so chastity is out the window." With respect to the encyclical *Humanae vitae*, far and wide, the document was discarded, rejected and even hated by many Catholics, even among some of the clergy. In fact, the Winnipeg Document was a forthright communication composed and approved by almost all the bishops of Canada defying the teaching of Pope St Paul VI in *Humanae vitae*.

Situation today

Now that close to sixty years have elapsed since *Humanae vitae* was published, increasing numbers of so-called followers of Christ have been distracted and fallen into the deep pit and quicksand of moral relativism, most specifically related to the encyclical and the reality of the use of contraception as immoral. As already remarked, never have we lived in a world with so much information. But never have we lived in a world with so much confusion, even on such serious moral matters as the means by which life should be allowed to enter into the world.

Distractions are many, but one of the most serious and pernicious distractions of the modern person is the belief that they have the right to choose life by whatever means they want, and even to end life in whatever time, manner or means they deem necessary.

6. Distracted by past hurts and resentments

We have all been hurt by others, and we have all hurt others, in many ways, times and circumstances. Wounds of the past not only distract us from living for God in the present moment but are a constant source of anxiety. To simply ignore these past hurts will never resolve the problem, much less heal the gaping wound that we have within us. As the saying goes: "Name it; claim it; then tame it!"

How can these past hurts and resentments be healed?

First of all, humbly admit that you have been hurt, perhaps deeply by others. Simply denying the reality of the hurt is like putting a sticking plaster over a gaping wound – there is no real possibility of healing.

Second, bring this wound to Jesus. Among the many titles given to Jesus is "Wounded Healer". In fact, it is by his wounds that we are healed. Once the wound is exposed and brought to Jesus, then the healing process can begin. Not only is Jesus our Wounded Healer, but he is also our Divine Physician.

Third, call to mind the people you have hurt in your life and from whom you have failed to ask forgiveness. Humble yourself and ask for forgiveness if they are living. If they aren't, pray for them. It is a good reminder that we are all sinners.

Fourth, beg Jesus for the grace to forgive the person or persons who have gravely wounded you.

This prayer is very pleasing to Jesus. It is very much related to the greatest attribute in the Sacred Heart of Jesus: his infinite mercy. One more helpful step is to say a prayer every day (even one "Hail Mary") for the person or persons who have hurt you. Surprisingly, this act of charity will redound to your benefit; it will ease your heart, help heal your wound and make it easier to forgive.

Fifth, call to mind some of the words of Jesus from the Sacred Text:

- From the cross: "Father, forgive them, for they know not what they are doing" (*Lk* 23:34).

- The Lord's Prayer: "Forgive us our trespasses as we forgive those who trespass against us" (*Mt* 6:12).

- In response to Peter's question on the number of times that we are obliged to forgive, and whether seven times would suffice: "I tell you, not seven times, but seventy-seven times" (*Mt* 18:21-22).

- His command: "Be merciful as your Heavenly Father is merciful" (*Lk* 6:36).

- The gift at the altar: "If you are approaching the altar with your gift and remember that your brother has something against you; leave your gift at the altar, be reconciled with your brother, then return to offer your gift" (*Mt* 5:23-24).

If forgiveness is still deemed difficult to the point of almost being impossible, let Jesus speak to your heart from the Sermon on the Mount. Read and meditate slowly on Matthew chapters 5, 6 and 7, focusing especially on 5:1-12 and 5:38-48.

Finally, be aware that what acid is to the intestines, so unresolved conflict, resentment and lack of forgiveness are to our soul. They can perforate, make holes and cause moral cancer.

How many people go through life with unforgiven wounds? How many are constantly, perpetually distracted from God, their family, and their work and other activities because they are a victim and slave of their own unwillingness to forgive past hurts and resentments?

In the words of the prophet Isaiah, Jesus actually came to "set the captives free". The captive set free can be you and can be me if we are willing, first, to beg God's mercy and forgiveness for hurting others, and second, to be merciful and forgiving towards those who have hurt us.

7. Distracted by constant worries

Do you worry? Has anyone ever called you a worryguts?
Are you a harbinger of gloom and doom? Are you a person
who expects the worst to befall you? Are you the type
who expects rain on the day of the picnic, even though
the weatherman has forecast blue skies and sunshine the
whole day? Do you not only cling to past hurts, but also
assume future hurts?

Many of us suffer from trust issues: we really and
honestly do not trust in God. Or if we do trust in God, we
do so only up to a certain point; then, our trust begins to
wane, and we start to vacillate and doubt.

One of the best remedies to conquer this constant
distraction of worrying about anything and everything,
but especially about the future and all that it has in store
for us, is to draw close to Jesus. We should beg for the
grace to sit at his feet like little, trusting children and
listen to his comforting words.

Read and meditate slowly on the Gospel of Matthew
chapters 5, 6 and 7. Focus especially upon 6:25-34, in
which Jesus repeats over and over again the command,
"Do not worry!" You might even divide his message into
the following points for reflection.

The birds of the air

To address our constant worrying for food, shelter and the
things of everyday living that we need, Jesus highlights

the example of the birds of the air. Never will you find a bird flying to a psychologist. Never will you meet a bird who is worrying about his next meal. We all, hopefully, see birds, and perhaps hear them, on a daily basis. They soar into the sky and swoop down into the fields; they sing songs that even the best-trained voices cannot imitate – especially the mocking bird. But never will we meet a depressed, worried or anxious bird on planet earth. Jesus invites us to ask ourselves this question: "If our Heavenly Father will provide for them, will he not provide for us, we of little faith?"

The flowers of the field

How much money we can waste in worldly, vain and even costly pursuits of new shoes, clothes, beauty treatments, etc! Yet Jesus reminds us that even King Solomon in all his costly array could not compare with the lilies of the field. If God clothes them with beauty day in and day out, will he not provide for us all that we need?

Jesus concludes by reminding us not to worry about the food that we will eat nor the clothes that we will wear. Why? Because that is what the pagans worry about. The following words of Jesus summarise the whole message and solution for our useless worries: "Seek first the Kingdom of God and his righteousness, and everything else will be given to you beside" (*Mt* 6:33).

Here are a few other words from Sacred Scripture that can help to alleviate the constant distraction that assails us when we worry excessively. Remember, God must be our fortress!

- "If God is with us, then who can be against us?" (*Rm* 8:31).

- "Our help is in the name of the Lord who made heaven and earth" (*Ps* 124:8).

- "When I am weak, it is then that I am strong" (*2 Co* 12:10).

- "The Lord is my Shepherd; there is nothing I shall lack" (*Ps* 23:1).

- "Behold I am with you always, even until the end of time" (*Mt* 28:20).

- "Heaven and earth will pass away, but my words will never pass away" (*Mt* 24:35).

- "In my Father's house there are many mansions. I go to prepare a place, a mansion for you. So that where I am, you also may be. If it were not so, I would not have told you so" (*Jn* 14:2-3).

- "Do not let your hearts be troubled and do not be afraid. For I have conquered the world" (*Jn* 14:27; 16:23).

- "If your faith were the size of a mustard seed, you could tell the mountain to move, and it would move" (*Mt* 17:20).

Have faith!

Ten-Step Programme to Conquer Distractions

We have examined seven of the many distractions that pull us away from God, who should be our primary focus: the devil, materialism, utilitarianism, religious indifferentism, and moral relativism, as well as holding on to past resentments and hurts, and worries and fears about the future. How then can we conquer these and the many other distractions that tend to assault us on a daily basis? In truth, we do not want to live a distracted, unfocused and fragmented life. The more we continue to live this way, the more we are cast into desolation.

Our end goal in life is to arrive at heaven, where we will have absolutely no distractions. There we will be contemplating the beatific vision of the Trinity – the Father, the Son and the Holy Spirit – with great joy for all eternity.

The question is how can we avoid being distracted and even sidetracked from the essential purpose of our life: to know and love God with all our heart, mind, body, soul and will, and to experience his tender love and care for us, now and for all eternity? In other words, we want God and his loving care for us to be the central focus of our time, energy and attention at all times.

The following Ten-Step Programme is offered as a strategy to help us to attain our goal. Let us discard all of the useless distractions in our lives and have the eyes of our soul focused on God and the good he desires for us here and now.

Step 1: General confession

Many people live a life of constant distraction, sadness and even depression, perhaps without even knowing why. One primary cause is guilt due to having unconfessed sins of the past. Unconfessed sin results in guilt, and with guilt come fears and depression; often, to assuage the guilt, many turn to vices. In Shakespeare's tragedy, *Macbeth*, Lady Macbeth is constantly portrayed as washing her hands – because of her guilt following the murder for which she and her husband were responsible. Shakespeare wrote: "Conscience does make cowards of all of us."

The making of a good 'general confession' of all the mortal sins of your life from the age of reason, whether confessed before or not, cannot be recommended strongly enough. One reason for this is the lack of good catechesis on confession for the past sixty years, so that many

Catholics have unconfessed mortal sins on their soul. There is a second reason, which the following question helps explain: "Looking back, do you have less sorrow for your past sins or more sorrow?" Most people answer "more" to this question because we are now more aware of how we hurt God, ourselves and others. A general confession is therefore a grace and a gift. Once you have made a general confession of all the sins of your life, you will find "the peace of God which surpasses all understanding" (*Ph* 4:7). Do not be surprised if the devil tries to sabotage your efforts; he knows the value of this more than we do.

These are the essential steps to prepare for and make a good confession:

1. *Examination of conscience.* This can be based on the Ten Commandments.

2. *Sorrow.* Have true sorrow for your sins, which have hurt the loving heart of Our Lord and Saviour, Jesus Christ.

3. *Firm purpose of amendment.* Have the firm purpose of not sinning again and of avoiding near occasions of sin.

4. *Confess your sins to the priest.* Confess your sins to the priest giving the number and kind of each mortal sin.

5. *Penance.* Carry out the penance the priest gives you straight away: it is the last step of confession.

Prepare well for your general confession, giving yourself a block of time, say a full morning, to write out your mortal sins using a good examination of conscience booklet, for example *Examination of Conscience* by Fr Robert Altier (available online). When confessing mortal sins, you must specify the kind of mortal sin and the number of times you committed that sin. Give your best estimate as to the number, then be at peace. God sees your good will. Do not rely on your memory but take your list with you to the confessional. You may confess behind the screen if you prefer anonymity. Read your sins aloud to the priest. Once the priest gives you absolution, do the penance the priest gives you right away, for that is the final step of any confession. Then, you will experience the true freedom of the sons and daughters of God. Later, should you remember one or more mortal sins that you forgot to confess, go to a priest and confess just the sin or sins that you forgot, receive absolution, do your penance, and again be at peace.

It must be said that not all priests are aware of the practice of a general confession, so ask ahead of time if they are familiar with it. Do not be surprised if they try to discourage you from making one, saying that you are not trusting in God's mercy. Do not argue with them, but simply look for another priest. What is more, due to there being fewer priests and confession hours these days, it is wise to make an appointment. If you have trouble finding a local priest or are concerned about anonymity, look for a large parish or cathedral where you are unknown and where there are more priests available. If there is a monastery in your area, ask if one of the monks is available to hear your general confession.

Jesus told St Faustina Kowalska that a good confession should have three basic qualities: transparency, humility and obedience. If you make your confession properly and with a sincere disposition, you can have no doubt that you are forgiven.

Having the firm conviction that Jesus, our merciful and loving Saviour, has forgiven us all of our sins is an infinite source of peace, joy and happiness, as well as a sure remedy to conquer the many distractions that assault us, some of which are likely to be related to escaping the guilt of our unconfessed sins of the past.

Step 2: Say no to sin

Once we have made a general confession of all the sins of our life, then, going forward, we must make a strong and firm decision to say NO to sin in all forms, shapes and sizes. St Dominic Savio made several promises at the time of his First Communion, including these three:

1. Jesus and Mary will be my best friends.

2. I will keep holy the Lord's Day and feast days.

3. Death rather than sin.

Sin indeed is the major obstacle, as well as a moral distraction in our daily lives. Many of us have become desensitised to sin because it has become commonplace.

St Ignatius of Loyola, in the *Spiritual Exercises*, offers us a powerful set of goals to aspire to:

1. death rather than commit one mortal sin
2. death rather than commit one deliberate venial sin
3. willingness to suffer humiliations for the sake of imitating Jesus all the more closely.

In our Ten-Step Programme, after making our general confession, let us resolve not to enter into any alliance with the devil or toy with sin in any form, size, shape or colour.

With that as our primary goal, we have a much greater possibility of avoiding mortal sin if we confess our sins frequently. Confession is both curative and preventive of sin. The late Fr Gabriele Amorth, former chief exorcist of the Vatican, said that we should confess at least every two weeks to fend off the enemy of our soul, the devil. That said, when we fall, we should get up and go to confession as soon as possible and begin again. God never tires of forgiving us; it is we who tire of asking for forgiveness.

Step 3: Live in the presence of God constantly

How easy it is to forget about God. How easy it is to become oblivious to God and his constant love for us.

How easy it is to be distracted and to focus on the non-essentials. How easy it is to become forgetful of what is sinful! A foolproof way to conquer the thousand distractions of life is to make a concerted effort to *live in the presence of God*. The seventeenth-century Parisian holy man of God, Brother Lawrence, claimed that his secret to growing in holiness and union with God was to strive to live constantly in God's presence.

St Teresa of Avila, the first female Doctor of the Church, stated that one of the primary reasons for committing sin is because we so easily forget about the presence of God. One of God's attributes is that God is omnipresent, meaning that no matter where we go, God is always present there. The psalmist reminds us: "If I ascend to the heavens, you are there; if I make my bed in the depths, you are there…. Even the darkness will not be dark to you; the night will shine like the day, for darkness is as light to you" (*Ps* 139:8-12). In the Acts of the Apostles, St Paul quotes a Greek poet: "As some of your poets have said, 'In him we live and move and have our being'" (*Ac*:17:28).

As a help to live in the presence of God, speckle your daily life with healthy reminders; we call these sacramentals. Wherever you find yourself, wherever you are living and working, have the following accompany you: statues or images of Jesus, his Mother Mary, St Joseph, and the angels and saints. Other powerful reminders are the crucifix, religious paintings, icons, stained-glass windows, medals of Mary and the saints, the Scapular and the Miraculous Medal, etc. All of these sacramentals are constant reminders that help us live in the presence of God. By living thus, the worldly, mundane, sensual and even sinful distractions that assail us can be reduced.

Step 4: Short prayers

Another tool to obviate distractions – one that was often used by the saints – is the habit of praying constantly by means of short prayers called aspirations or ejaculations. It is a sure means to enkindle the fire of God's love within our hearts. There are many such short prayers, but the following are a few that can prove exceedingly useful:

"Sacred Heart of Jesus, have mercy on me."

"Jesus, I trust in you."

"Sweet Heart of Mary, be my salvation."

"Lord, save me."

"Lord, strengthen my faith."

"Lord, come to my aid."

"Lord, make haste to help me."

"The Lord is my Shepherd, there is nothing I shall want."

"Jesus, Mary, and Joseph, I love you, save souls."

Step 5: Solid and orthodox spiritual reading

Those who are pursuing a life of holiness have always been encouraged to form the habit of applying their minds to solid, orthodox spiritual reading. Begin, of course, with the Bible, the Word of God. Next, read about the lives of the saints. The saints are our friends in heaven, and they are very much alive. Ask for intercessory prayers from the saints you have been named after, or whose name you chose for your Confirmation, or those you have come to know and love through reading or seeing films about. Look up new saints and learn about them. Try to imitate their virtues. Ask them to pray for you and with you for your loved ones here on earth, especially those who are suffering or those who are living lives far from God. Finally, find a good, solid book on the Blessed Virgin Mary, so as to enkindle your love for her. You cannot go wrong with the classic work by St Alphonsus Liguori, *The Glories of Mary*. It is true that Mary is Queen of heaven and earth, but as St Thérèse reminds us, "Mary is more Mother than Queen." May we always love and cherish Mary as our mother.

By applying your mind to a daily diet of solid spiritual reading, the cobwebs of mundane and earthly distractions will dissipate like the dew exposed to the morning sun. In short: to counteract the many worldly distractions that we are constantly bombarded with, we must neutralise it by solid spiritual reading.

Step 6: Spiritual direction

Let us be honest: we all have many blind spots in our spiritual lives. Even the best of us, on the best of days, do not always clearly see the hand of God, the face of God, nor the will of God in our daily lives. There are three views of the human person: the way others see us, the way we see ourselves, and the way God sees us. The first two are somewhat erroneous; God's view of us is the true and authentic one. By means of the systematic, methodical and orderly assistance of a trained spiritual director, we can see ourselves in a more clear and objective light.

Many of the saints are adamant about the need to have a good spiritual director. Among these are St Teresa of Avila, St John of the Cross and St Ignatius of Loyola. That said, it is not always easy to find a spiritual director, but bear in mind that spiritual direction does not require a face-to-face, in person relationship. It can take place over the phone or by video call. Pray that God will help you find a good and well-trained spiritual director. As with general confession, you should find out if a local parish priest provides spiritual direction; try a large parish or cathedral where there are more priests available; or even check for monasteries in your area and ask if they provide spiritual direction. If you cannot find a suitable spiritual director, then do as the insistent widow in the Gospel did: pray earnestly to Jesus and Our Blessed Mother every day to help you find a good spiritual director!

This could be one of the greatest blessings and treasures of your life, not least because it is a sure means to conquer worldly and sinful distractions.

Step 7: The daily holy hour

Venerable Fulton J. Sheen paid great attention to God in his life as priest, bishop, writer, radio evangelist, TV evangelist, and missionary. In more than fifty years of his life as a priest and a bishop, amidst the many temptations, distractions, and heavy loads and crosses he experienced, this great man of God never missed his daily holy hour. He made this time with the Lord in front of the most Blessed Sacrament his priority every day. He called this his "Daily Holy Hour – the Hour of Power!"

Following in the footsteps of this great man of God and making the commitment to make a daily holy hour can be a most efficacious means to be aware of God's presence during the course of our day. Use the prayer method *lectio divina* explained in the penultimate chapter entitled "Praying *Lectio Divina*" (pp69-72). The daily hour of prayer, during which time we read and meditate on Holy Scripture, listen to Our Lord speaking to us, and then talk with him, can help us to resist the many temptations of the enemy, can curb our curiosity, and can help us focus on doing everything during the course of our day for the greater honour and glory of Almighty God.

How easy it is to spend time, effort and energy on our phone, computer, laptop, iPad, etc. How many hours do we spend on these electronic devices that might even be harmful to us? Would it not be more profitable for us to give to the Lord Jesus at least one hour every day – the Hour of Power? In return, we can be sure that Our Lord, who can never be outdone in generosity, will pour abundant graces upon us.

When giving retreats for priests and bishops, Sheen would point out to them that often when they preached and talked, people would not listen. However, when he, Sheen, spoke, all would listen. The reason? Once again, the Hour of Power. The purpose is simply to spend the holy hour looking at Jesus, listening to Jesus, talking to Jesus and unloading your heart to Jesus. Then, as a consequence, Jesus will be at the centre of your heart and your day! Jesus invites us in these words: "Come to me all of you who are weary, and I will give you rest. Take my yoke upon you and learn from me because I am meek and humble of heart. My yoke is easy and my burden is light" (*Mt* 11:28-30).

Step 8: Remember why you are here and where you are going

It is so easy for us to be distracted by things that are not of God. Never do I tire of striving to promote authentic Ignatian spirituality and the starting point of the *Spiritual Exercises*, what Ignatius of Loyola calls the "First Principle and Foundation". If we consider this reflection, even briefly, every day, this will keep us on the straight and narrow path that will lead us safely to our goal, which is heaven. Listen and reflect calmly and prayerfully on these words of Ignatius: "We are created to praise God, to reverence God, to serve God and by means of that to save our souls" (*Spiritual Exercises* # 23). Even if we were to reflect upon these words for a minute a day, that would help us direct our mind, will and energies to attain the goal of eternal life. How easy it is for us to be distracted and sidetracked by the pursuit of money, power, pleasure, sexual pleasure and honours. How pervasive, pernicious and poisonous are those attractions, and how many choose them over God!

Step 9: Friends

St Paul writes that: "Bad company corrupts good morals" (*1 Co* 15:33). Aristotle insists on the importance of social relationships, stating that man is truly a social animal. It is therefore important who our friends are. It is not uncommon in the lives of the saints to see how one saint had a positive influence on another. St John Bosco helped Dominic Savio on his path to sainthood. If it had not been for the prayers of St Monica, we would not have had the conversion of St Augustine. At times, it even runs in the family: St Thérèse of Lisieux had parents who are now canonised saints – Louis and Zélie Martin – and St Bernard of Clairvaux was surrounded by a cluster of family members who became saints. What we are alluding to with respect to friends is the paramount importance of true and authentic friends in helping us to avoid falling prey to the pernicious distractions of the world that tug us into sin, the sinful patterns and the vices that endanger the salvation of our immortal souls. Such friends will help us follow the paths of the saints who have gone before us.

When dealing with young teenagers – Confirmation students aged thirteen to sixteen – I encourage them to have friends and to cultivate wholesome friendships. Then I ask them: "What is the most important quality of an authentic friend?" Often, they will respond: "A friend is faithful at all times." Not good enough! Thieves, gang members and bank robbers are faithful even in their sordid and dastardly deeds. A true friend of yours will be a bridge for you to deepen your friendship with Jesus – the one true friend who will never fail you, never let you down.

Let us step back and examine our friends. Are they a bridge by which our friendship with Jesus is being bolstered and fortified? Or are they an obstacle or barricade to our union with him? A true friend will not distract us from Jesus. Quite the contrary: they will help us to focus our eyes and attention on him.

Step 10: Mary – our life, our sweetness and our hope

There is one person whom God created who at every moment of her existence, in all times and places, never took her gaze off Jesus. He was the very centre and meaning of her existence. Pope St John Paul II, in his apostolic letter, *The Blessed Virgin Mary and the Rosary* (*Rosarium Virginis Mariae*), points out that Mary had her eyes focused on Jesus at all times. Mary contemplated Jesus, the Incarnate Word, even before he was born, as he developed in her womb. In Bethlehem, she contemplated the Baby Jesus in her arms. Mary contemplated Jesus as a young boy in the family home in Nazareth and in the carpenter's shop as he worked side by side with St Joseph. During his public ministry, Mary sat next to Jesus at the wedding feast at Cana and led him to perform his first public miracle, the turning of water into wine. Then she gave us the best advice ever (the last words of Mary recorded in the Gospels): "Do whatever he tells you" (*Jn* 2:5). Finally, as Jesus hung from the cross and was about to breathe forth his spirit, he left his Mother Mary to his best friend, the apostle St John, and in that moment, to us as well. "Woman, behold thy son; son, behold thy mother" (*Jn* 19:26-27). Our Lady of Sorrows bore Jesus's suffering and death on the cross with a mother's love for our eternal salvation.

Finally, according to long Catholic tradition, Jesus rose from the dead and made several appearances.

Though the event is not recorded in Sacred Scripture, the Catholic Church maintains that the first appearance of the Risen Lord Jesus was to his mother, Mary. After Jesus's suffering on the cross, Mary's suffering was the greatest. However, when Jesus rose from the dead, no one's joy was greater than the joy of his loving, and now joyful, Mother Mary.

Following the exhortation of the great Doctor of the Church, St Bernard, the Mellifluous Doctor, let us gently lift our eyes, our gaze, our mind and our heart to Mary, who is invoked as *Stella Maris*, Star of the Sea. In the midst of the many storms and tempests of life, let us lift our gaze on high to Mary. Sailors are led safely to shore by following the Star of the Sea. May Mary, *Stella Maris*, lead us safely to heaven, our eternal home: "*Stella Maris*, lead us gently, firmly, and lovingly into the presence of Jesus who is the Light of the World and our eternal salvation. Amen."

Frequently Asked Questions about Obstacles to Prayer

Q *"I can't pray because I have ADHD. I literally cannot sit still or focus my mind."*

Admittedly, that is difficult, but be assured that *you can pray*, and you will be able to follow most of my Ten-Step Programme, even with ADHD. I want to encourage you with this thought: Our Lady of Fatima appeared to three shepherd children in 1917 and told them that souls are going to hell because there is no one to pray and suffer for them. So, each day, offer your prayer and the sufferings you experience with ADHD to Our Blessed Mother for the saving of souls. Only in heaven will you know how many souls were saved because of you.

You just need to find ways to pray that work for you. Here is some helpful advice. To begin with, if you make no other prayer at all, beg Jesus for the grace to pray. That is a prayer in itself, and it is very pleasing to Jesus. Second, develop strategies to "distract your distractions".

Pray while taking a walk, and if you notice the beauty of nature while walking, that in itself is a prayer of praise. Do you need something in your hands, such as a rosary? That's perfectly fine. Think of holding the rosary beads in your hand as holding the hand of Mary! Maybe you need to have a short prayer to bring you back the very instant you notice your mind wandering or notice yourself starting to do something besides praying. Something as simple as, "Lord, I love you; help me to pray" or, "Mother Mary, pray for me" will do. If you have to pray these a thousand times, that is very pleasing to Jesus and Mary. Above all, keep going, and do not be discouraged. Jesus is very pleased with you and your efforts, and he will shower you with graces.

Q *"I can't pray because I am a busy parent and my children take all of my attention. I am not so much distracted in prayer as focused on them."*

Naturally, you need to take care of your children, but that does not mean that you cannot pray. In fact, one of your jobs as a parent is to teach your children to pray, to pray with them and to pray for them. Have a prayer you say together when you get up in the morning, say grace before every meal and have a prayer you pray before leaving the house together. In fact, let your children see you putting prayer before everything else. For example, "I know we are running late, but we are still going to take one more minute to pray before we leave to ask God to be with us and bring us all home safely." End the day by saying prayers with them at bedtime.

There are two more very important ways to bring prayer into your home.

First, as many days as possible, take fifteen to twenty minutes after dinner or before bedtime to pray the Rosary as a family. Our Lady of Fatima told the three children of Fatima to pray the Rosary daily for the salvation of souls. Venerable Patrick Peyton promoted the family Rosary, saying, "The Family that prays together, stays together." In the movie *Pray: The Story of Patrick Peyton*, former Major League Baseball player Mike Sweeney describes how his marriage was on the rocks when he and his wife were encouraged to start praying the family Rosary – which he believes saved the marriage and the family.

During the Rosary, involve your children: let each child pray a decade and say their own intention for that decade. Remind them that this is a great act of charity. Only God knows how many souls will be saved because of your daily Rosary. That was the promise of Our Lady when she appeared at Fatima.

Second, purchase a children's Bible of the Old and New Testaments, and for half an hour on Sundays get the children to take turns reading aloud a Bible story. There are stories of great heroes in the Old Testament. The Gospels are about Jesus, what he is asking of us, and all that he did on earth for the love of us. An activity such as this helps their reading skills and their confidence in reading aloud before others and makes God come alive for them. The more they know and learn about God as children, the stronger their faith will be as they get older.

Make your children, your household tasks and your family time together be the reason you pray, rather than the reason you don't. The more you do this, the more natural it will become for your mind to turn to God, rather than your phone or the TV in your spare moments.

Q *"I can't pray because I have a demanding job/I'm too busy with my studies. Work/school takes all my time, and if I take time out, I won't be any good at my job/studies, and I will fall behind or even get fired/fail my classes."*

This is your personal experience of the seven distractions I talked about in the fourth chapter. It is the devil telling you that your job or schooling is the most important thing, which you accept, because your mind works in a fundamentally utilitarian way, meaning that your value and self-worth depend on how much you produce, fostered by materialism – how many goods and honours of this world you can accumulate and enjoy. The decision to put God before all else is the most radical one you will ever make, but in another way it should be the easiest, because everything good in our lives is made better through a deepening relationship with God. If your job, education or other commitments truly prevent you from praying, the question is not whether you should pray, but whether your work and schooling will bring you true happiness – not just in the next life, but even in this life.

St Augustine chased honours, riches and sensual pleasures for the first thirty-one years of his life and was never satisfied. Only when he surrendered his life to Christ was his heart satisfied: "You have made us for yourself, O Lord, and our hearts are restless until they rest in You."

A good reflection would be to weigh the material things and the pleasures of this short life on earth, on the one hand, against eternity, which is for ever and ever, on the other hand. Jesus said: "Not everyone who says to me, 'Lord, Lord' will enter the kingdom of heaven, but only the one who does the will of my Father who is in heaven" (*Mt* 7:21).

Q *"I can't pray because I don't know what to say, so I just end up thinking about other things."*

You are not alone in this! Learning to pray is like learning a new language. It takes effort and discipline, and a good prayer method that is suitable to us.

Most people don't know what to say; that is why there are different prayer methods. Two are introduced in this book. The penultimate chapter presents a classical method of prayer encouraged by Pope Benedict XVI called *lectio divina* (see "Praying *Lectio divina*, pp69-72), teaching us how to pray with Scripture, and when we pray with the Gospels, how to enter into the life of Christ and become present to him and he to us.

"Building a House of Prayer in Our Soul" (pp73-79) gives us a second method of prayer building on *lectio divina* by introducing Ignatian Contemplation given to us by St Ignatius of Loyola. In this prayer, praying with the Gospels, we are attentive to all the scenes in the life of Jesus and we imagine being present at these events – his birth, his private life, his public life of preaching, healing, and casting out demons, his suffering and death on the cross, his glorious resurrection.

As an example, imagine yourself being present when Jesus is born in the stable of Bethlehem – see the poverty of the stable, the humility of Mary and Joseph making the best of these surroundings, the humble and lowly shepherds who are the first to adore the Lord of lords and the King of kings! You are there, you are part of all this, and your heart is filled with awe and wonder. When you are more experienced in this type of prayer, you may find Mary offering you the baby Jesus to hold and adore in your arms.

Picture another scene – stand with Mary, John, and Magdalene beneath the cross. Jesus is nailed to the cross, his body covered with blood from the deep wounds of the scourging, his face covered with blood from the crown of sharp thorns on his head, for an agonising three long hours! St Ignatius assures us that if you were the only person in the world who needed to be saved, Jesus would have suffered and died on the cross for your eternal salvation!

As Mary stands beneath the cross, Jesus says: "Woman, behold your son"… and to John, "Behold your mother" (*Jn* 19:26-27). By giving Mary to John, Jesus is giving Mary to each and every one us to be our mother! What are you thinking? What are you feeling? Knowing that Jesus is giving you his own mother to be your mother, to watch over you and guide you, to pray for you? Knowing that Mary is willingly enduring her great suffering in Jesus's death on the cross for your eternal salvation?

A second and essential component of practising Ignatian Contemplation is bringing to Jesus your own needs, desires, concerns and wounds. Jesus is the wounded healer! He will comfort and console you in all your trials, and help you discern your path of true happiness in life. Open up to him, talk to him, let his love and concern for you be like a sweet balm on your heart.

In addition to this method of prayer, Ignatius teaches us how to have an ordered prayer life. This is discussed in "Building a House of Prayer in Our Soul" (pp73-79). He gives the reasons to pray, how to pray, when to pray, how often to pray, what to pray, how to handle dryness in prayer, how to get back when we lapse in prayer, ways to see the fruits of our prayer over time, and so much more.

Once we learn to pray using Ignatian Contemplation with Jesus in the Gospels, we will find that the whole of Sacred Scripture, both the Old Testament and New Testament, open up to us in a wonderful way for Ignation Contemplation in prayer!

What is clear, is that Jesus is calling each one of us to enter into "the one thing necessary" – a deep, intimate friendship with him through prayer, and not sometimes, or when we feel like it, but all the days of our life!

Q *"What do I do when I encounter dryness in prayer?"* Dryness is a form of suffering in prayer that we all experience for a variety of reasons. Here are a few of those reasons and some suggested remedies.

First, having unconfessed mortal sins means that we are no longer in a state of grace, which blocks our friendship with Jesus and inhibits our prayer life. Examine your conscience and ask yourself, "Have I committed serious sins that remain unconfessed?" The remedy, of course, is to confess any mortal sins to a priest as soon as possible, restoring grace and peace to our soul and our friendship with Jesus.

However, even venial sins, especially repeated ones – such as gossiping, using bad language, overeating, telling small lies, harbouring a grudge, and scandalising others by our dress, speech or actions, to name but a few – can cause dryness in prayer. For this reason, though not required, the confession of venial sins as well as mortal sins is encouraged by the Church. The grace of confession is curative and preventive. It makes us conscious of these smaller sins and gives us the grace to overcome them.

Second, being overworked or overtired can bring about dryness in prayer. If this is how you are feeling, it is best to pray a Rosary for the salvation of souls and catch up on your sleep. Then, start afresh again when your strength is restored. However, if this is a recurring pattern, examine your life. Make a list of your daily activities and prayerfully decide what has to go so that you can be faithful to prayer, your daily conversation with Jesus, who will always provide all you need if you place your trust in him.

Third, sickness or illness can bring about dryness in prayer. In this case, our suffering is doubled by the very fact that we cannot pray.

Short aspirations can help, for example, "Jesus, make haste to help me!"; "Jesus, I love you"; "Jesus, I trust in you"; "Mary, Mother of Perpetual Help, help me now." It is important that you call your parish to see if a Eucharistic Minister is available to bring you Holy Communion. To the extent that you are able, do passive things. Watch or listen to the Mass online. Listen to the Rosary recited on the radio. Have peaceful religious music playing in the background. All these things can ease your pain and bring peace to your soul. Finally, and of paramount importance, remember to join your sufferings to the sufferings of Jesus on the cross for the salvation of souls, especially those of your loved ones who have strayed far from the Church.

Finally, dryness in prayer can be a suffering sent from God for our purification and sanctification. In this case, persevere in prayer! We know by faith that we are present to Jesus, even when we cannot feel his presence. This is a matter of faith and trust in Jesus built on a foundation of daily prayer. And our prayer is even more fruitful *because* we are not getting anything out of it. Again, remember to offer this suffering for the salvation of immortal souls, as Our Lady of Fatima taught the three children of Fatima to do. Only in heaven will we know how many souls were saved because of the suffering we offered for them.

Praying *Lectio Divina*

———————

Pope Benedict XVI encouraged us to go deeper in our prayer life using a classical method, *lectio divina*. The retired pontiff strongly exhorted followers of Christ to utilise the Word of God as fertile ground for delving into the depths of prayer.

My intention in this short chapter is to set out the steps the Holy Father suggests – and a touch more – to motivate us to never tire in growing in our union with God through a deeper prayer life. Prayer has no limits given that prayer is union with an eternal and infinite God.

These are the steps:

Step 1: *Lectio*

Open the text you have chosen to meditate upon and read it. However, before reading, ask Our Blessed Mother Mary to pray with you and pray for you. Then, invite the Holy Spirit, known as the Interior Master, to help you in prayer. Now the prayer of the young Samuel can be yours: "Speak, O Lord, for your servant is listening."

(*1 S* 3:10) What a privilege you have – God wants to speak to your heart!

Step 2: *Meditatio*

Now apply the use of your memory and understanding to know what God is trying to say to you through this text. Rejoice in the fact that God, right now, has a special message he wants to communicate to you through this reading and meditation. Be open to God; think and pray. Be bold enough to ask the Lord: "Lord God, exactly what is the message you want to communicate to me in my heart and my life right now?" He will hear you and respond.

Step 3: *Contemplatio*

Now utilise another mental faculty that God has endowed you with in penetrating this text, namely the use of your imagination. We all have an imagination – maybe even a very vivid imagination! However, the imagination is like a double-edged sword: it can be used for good or for evil. The imagination used for good might be for you to imagine walking side by side with Jesus the Good Shepherd (*Ps* 23; *Jn* 10:1-18), contemplating the loving gaze of the Good Shepherd peering into your eyes, hearing his gentle and reassuring voice, and experiencing the strong but loving embrace of his arm around your weary shoulders. In summary, your imagination must be trained in the pursuit of good.

Step 4: *Oratio*

Now you have arrived at the very heart of the essence and purpose of *lectio divina*, which is *oratio*, meaning prayer. At any time during your reading of the chosen text, when your mind or imagination sparks an idea that descends to your heart, it is time to open up in prayer. This means that you open up your heart and talk to the Lord in the most simple, trusting and intimate way about what you are thinking, feeling, experiencing. Our Lord is never too busy for you, and he is always ready and willing to listen to you when you decide to talk to him. This conversation with the Lord during your time of prayer can be for a few minutes, half an hour, an hour – whatever length the good Lord inspires in the depths of your heart. Then, continue reading the text until your heart is moved again, or until the time you have allotted for prayer is over.

Step 5: *Actio*

Authentic prayer must translate into the reality of your life. Doctor of the Church St Teresa of Avila made this acute observation. The acid test to prove our prayer is authentic is how our prayer is manifested in our life. Jesus himself reminds us that we can tell the tree by its fruit. A good tree brings forth good fruit; a bad tree, bad fruit. If we are truly praying with sincerity, honesty, rectitude of intention and love for God, we will begin to see good fruit or virtues growing in our life. Over time, from the tree of our life will blossom and flourish the following: faith, hope, humility, purity, meekness, patience, obedience, self-control, mortification, fortitude and, finally, charity, the Queen of all the virtues according to St Thomas Aquinas, which "binds everything together in perfect harmony" (*Col* 3:14). Our Lady is our example at all times. In the Annunciation, we see Mary as a contemplative. In the Visitation, after her time of prayer, we see Mary going in haste to bring the fruit of her prayer in service to her cousin Elizabeth. May Our Lady's example motivate us to also become *contemplatives in action.*

Step 6: *Transformatio*

Indeed, if our *lectio divina* is true and authentic, we will see a gradual transformation in our daily lives. In our prayer life, our aim should be to implement the words of the great apostle St Paul: "It is no longer I who live, but Christ who lives in me" (*Ga* 2:20). This is the ultimate goal of *lectio divina* and all authentic prayer: knowing, loving and imitating Jesus Christ, following in his footsteps, and ultimately, transformation into his very essence and being.

What are you waiting for? Why not start your *lectio divina* today? Choose your text; read it, meditate on it, contemplate it, pray it; live it out and allow God, through the working of the Holy Spirit, to transform you into the saint that he has created you to be.

Building a House of Prayer
in Our Soul

───────────

We need a blueprint to build a house; we also need a blueprint to build a house of prayer within our soul. St Ignatius of Loyola gives us this blueprint in the Prayer of Ignatian Contemplation.

"The glory of God is man fully alive", according to St Irenaeus. The human person is composed of body and soul. We are both physical and spiritual beings, and both need to be nourished if we are to become fulfilled human beings. We nourish our spiritual life through prayer. Or, using another analogy, what air is to the lungs, prayer is to the soul.

If you are reading this book, the assumption is that you already have a prayer life or at least that you desire to have one.

Let us start with Scripture, the Word of God that speaks to us in all the circumstances of our lives. Martha and Mary were two sisters who lived with their brother,

Lazarus, in Bethany. Jesus and his disciples were always welcome to visit this family who loved him very much.

Mary, the more contemplative or prayerful one by nature, would sit at the feet of Jesus listening to him. Martha, the more active one, would busy herself preparing a meal for their guests to enjoy. On one occasion, Martha decided to speak up.

Let us read the following passage of Sacred Scripture (*Lk* 10:38-42) to see what happened:

> As Jesus and his disciples were on their way, he came to a village where a woman named Martha opened her home to him. She had a sister called Mary, who sat at the Lord's feet listening to what he said. But Martha was distracted by all the preparations that had to be made. She came to him and asked, "Lord, don't you care that my sister has left me to do the work by myself? Tell her to help me!" "Martha, Martha," the Lord answered, "you are worried and upset about many things, but few things are needed – or indeed only one. Mary has chosen what is better, and it will not be taken away from her."

Jesus is calling each one of us to enter into "the one thing necessary" – a deep, intimate friendship with him through prayer. Friendship is based on getting to know someone by spending time with that person. With Jesus, the most important friendship in our lives, St Ignatius of

Loyola says to give him an hour a day. Spend one hour a day with Jesus and he will bless the other twenty-three hours of your day! If, in all honesty, you cannot pray one hour a day, then make a commitment to pray at least thirty minutes a day to establish this intimate friendship with Jesus. Why do we do this? Because it is Jesus who is calling us to himself so that we can avoid sin and practise virtue and he can help us through the trials and sufferings of this life until we rejoice with him for ever in heaven! As a bonus, by the graces we earn and the example we give, our daily hour of prayer helps us bring many others to heaven with us. Especially those whom we love and pray for, who do not pray for themselves.

We will now address two key elements of our daily holy hour, namely praying with Scripture and bringing to the Lord the concerns that are heavy on our mind and heart. However, when you are reading Scripture or talking with Jesus about your life, it's important to stay with a thought that captivates you. Stay where your heart is until you feel ready to move on. Our Lord never tires of spending this time of loving friendship with you. On the other hand, if you are reading Scripture or talking to Jesus and you are not getting much out of it – we all hit dry spots – stay for the whole hour anyway and make it an offering of love to Our Lord. Prayer is a decision, not a feeling. Our Lord cannot be outdone in generosity, and he will shower you with blessings for your perseverance.

Finally, after each holy hour, take a few minutes to write in a journal your key experience in prayer that day. It will help you to see over time how your relationship with Jesus has grown. However, if you miss one day, or even more, simply begin again. Do not try to make it up by doing two holy hours a day. That is a temptation of the devil that will discourage you and make you give up prayer.

Let God speak to you

The first element of praying your holy hour is listening to the Word of God – Sacred Scripture. This is God himself speaking to you. Start by reading the Gospels, the life and teachings of Our Lord and Saviour, Jesus Christ. Each Gospel has something special to offer. For example, the Gospel of Luke is generally known as 'the mercy Gospel'. In addition, Luke starts with the infancy narratives, the births of John the Baptist and Jesus.

For one hour a day, read the Gospel narrative and think about how the words and happenings in the life of Jesus speak to you. You may even try imagining that you are present in certain scenes of the Gospel. This is 'Ignatian contemplation'. In the Gospel of Luke, you might imagine that you follow the shepherds going to see Jesus born in the stable of Bethlehem, and there you see Jesus in the arms of Mary. Imagine Mary handing you the baby Jesus to hold. What are you thinking, what are you feeling, holding the Saviour of the world in your arms?

After praying with the Gospels, you can read and pray with the Acts of the Apostles, also known as the Gospel of the Holy Spirit, to see how the Church that Jesus established grew after Pentecost. Peter gave a sermon, and three thousand were converted. The witness and blood of the first martyr, St Stephen, led to the conversion of St Paul.

In the Old Testament, pray with the Psalms. They capture all the thoughts and emotions of the human person and can bring great comfort to us. There are great stories of faith and courage to be found in the Old Testament, too. The book of Genesis, chapters 37-50, tells the story of Joseph, son of Jacob, who is a Christ figure. The book of Tobit is a charming story of God's intervention through the Archangel Raphael in the lives of two suffering servants of the Lord, Sarah and Tobit. The book of Esther is the story of a queen willing to risk her life for the salvation of God's people. Isaiah speaks about the "suffering servant", a prophecy of the life and death of Jesus.

As often as we read and pray with the Scriptures, the Word of God speaks to us in a different way, because we are different. Delve into the richness of God's Word! Let it enter deep into your heart and help you ponder the story of your life, and how God is calling you to love and to serve others.

Talk to the Lord

The second element of praying your holy hour is talking with Jesus about what is happening in your daily life – your joys and sorrows, hopes and dreams, worries and sufferings. Place them in the Sacred Heart of Jesus, pierced for love of you. What is on your mind and heart right now? Talk with Jesus about this. He hears you, he sees you, he loves you, and he will help you by giving you what is the greatest good for you in your life right now. We do not always see it that way. However, if we are honest, looking back over our life, we can see that he was always working on our behalf, through the good things, as well as the hard things that helped us become the person he created us to be. His plans are always better and greater. Lord, we praise you and we bless you! Help us to stay by your side always by means of our daily holy hour, our "Hour of Power" as Venerable Fulton J. Sheen called it.

If after reading my recommendations for improving your prayer life you still believe that you are too busy to spend one hour a day with Our Lord, or at least thirty minutes a day, then maybe you are too busy. Let us be honest: our work is never done. Consider this maybe another distraction of the devil so that we will miss the greater good: a deep and abiding friendship with Jesus through the time we spend with him in our daily holy hour. Let us resolve to defeat the enemy of our soul by being faithful to our daily conversation and growing friendship with Jesus. Fortified in his love and grace, we are able to turn our good-will and resources with greater love and charity to the needs of others, those whom God places in our lives, and he will bless our efforts with even more abundant fruits.